W9-BGZ-162

THE EVERYTHING KIDS' MORE AMAZING MAZES BOOK

Wind your way through hours of adventurous fun!

Beth L. Blair and Jennifer A. Ericsson

Aadamsmedia

Avon, Massachusetts

PUBLISHER Karen Cooper

DIRECTOR OF ACQUISITIONS AND INNOVATION Paula Munier

MANAGING EDITOR, EVERYTHING® SERIES Lisa Laing

COPY CHIEF Casey Ebert

ACQUISITIONS EDITOR Katrina Schroeder

ASSOCIATE DEVELOPMENT EDITOR Hillary Thompson

SENIOR DEVELOPMENT EDITOR Brett Palana-Shanahan

EDITORIAL ASSISTANT Ross Weisman

EVERYTHING® SERIES COVER DESIGNER Erin Alexander

LAYOUT DESIGNERS Colleen Cunningham, Elisabeth Lariviere, Ashley Vierra, Denise Wallace

Copyright © 2010 by F+W Media, Inc.
All rights reserved.
This book, or parts thereof, may not be reproduced in any form without permission from the publisher; exceptions are made for brief excerpts used in published reviews and photocopies made for classroom use.

An Everything® Series Book.
Everything® and everything.com® are registered trademarks of F+W Media, Inc.

Published by Adams Media, a division of F+W Media, Inc.
57 Littlefield Street, Avon, MA 02322. U.S.A.
www.adamsmedia.com

ISBN 10: 1-4405-0150-5
ISBN 13: 978-1-4405-0150-0
eISBN 10: 1-4405-0151-3
eISBN 13: 978-1-4405-0151-7

Printed by RR Donnelley, Owensville, MO, US

10 9 8 7 6 5 4 3 2 1

April 2010

This publication is designed to provide accurate and authoritative information with regard to the subject matter covered. It is sold with the understanding that the publisher is not engaged in rendering legal, accounting, or other professional advice. If legal advice or other expert assistance is required, the services of a competent professional person should be sought.

—From a *Declaration of Principles* jointly adopted by a Committee of the American Bar Association and a Committee of Publishers and Associations

Many of the designations used by manufacturers and sellers to distinguish their products are claimed as trademarks. When those designations appear in this book and Adams Media was aware of a trademark claim, the designations have been printed with initial capital letters.

Interior illustrations by Kurt Dolber.
Puzzles by Beth L. Blair.

This book is available at quantity discounts for bulk purchases.
For information, please call 1-800-289-0963.

Visit the entire Everything® series at www.everything.com

Contains material adapted and abridged from:

The Everything® Kids' Animal Puzzle and Activity Book by Beth L. Blair and Jennifer A. Ericsson, copyright © 2005 by F+W Media, Inc., ISBN 13: 978-1-59337-305-4, ISBN 10: 1-59337-305-8.

The Everything® Kids' Baseball Book, 5th Edition by Greg Jacobs, copyright © 2008 by F+W Media, Inc., ISBN 13: 978-1-59869-487-1, ISBN 10: 1-59869-487-1.

The Everything® Kids' Christmas Puzzle and Activity Book by Beth L. Blair and Jennifer A. Ericsson, copyright © 2003 by F+W Media, Inc., ISBN 13: 978-1-58062-965-2, ISBN 10: 1-58062-965-2.

The Everything® Kids' Crazy Puzzles Book by Beth L. Blair and Jennifer A. Ericsson, copyright © 2005 by F+W Media, Inc., ISBN 13: 978-1-59337-631-0, ISBN 10: 1-59337-361-9.

The Everything® Kids' Dinosaurs Book by Kathi Wagner and Sheryl Racine, copyright © 2005 by F+W Media, Inc., ISBN 13: 978-1-59337-360-3, ISBN 10: 1-59337-360-0.

The Everything® Kids' Environment Book by Sheri Amsel, copyright © 2007 by F+W Media, Inc., ISBN 13: 978-1-59869-670-7, ISBN 10: 1-59869-670-X.

The Everything® Kids' Football Book by Greg Jacobs, copyright © 2008 by F+W Media, Inc., ISBN 13: 978-1-59869-565-6, ISBN 10: 1-59869-565-7.

The Everything® Kids' Gross Mazes Book by Beth L. Blair, copyright © 2008 by F+W Media, Inc., ISBN 13: 978-1-59337-616-1, ISBN 10: 1-59337-616-2.

The Everything® Kids' Halloween Puzzle and Activity Book by Beth L. Blair and Jennifer A. Ericsson, copyright © 2003 by F+W Media, Inc., ISBN 13: 978-1-58062-959-1, ISBN 10: 1-58062-959-8.

The Everything® Kids' Hanukkah Puzzle and Activity Book by Beth L. Blair and Jennifer A. Ericsson, copyright © 2008 by F+W Media, Inc., ISBN 13: 978-1-59869-788-9, ISBN 10: 1-59869-788-9.

The Everything® Kids' Horses Book by Kathi Wagner and Sheryl Racine, copyright © 2006 by F+W Media, Inc., ISBN 13: 978-1-59337-608-6, ISBN 10: 1-59337-608-1.

The Everything® Kids' Mazes Book by Beth L. Blair, copyright © 2001 by F+W Media, Inc., ISBN 13: 978-1-58062-558-6, ISBN 10: 1-58062-558-4.

The Everything® Kids' Mummies, Pharaohs, and Pyramids Puzzle and Activity Book by Beth L. Blair and Jennifer A. Ericsson, copyright © 2008 by F+W Media, Inc., ISBN 13: 978-1-59869-797-1, ISBN 10: 1-59869-797-8.

The Everything® Kids' Pirates Puzzle and Activity Book by Beth L. Blair and Jennifer A. Ericsson, copyright © 2006 by F+W Media, Inc., ISBN 13: 978-1-59337-607-9, ISBN 10: 1-59337-607-3.

The Everything® Kids' Racecars Puzzle and Activity Book by Beth L. Blair and Jennifer A. Ericsson, copyright © 2008 by F+W Media, Inc., ISBN 13: 978-1-59869-243-3, ISBN 10: 1-59869-243-7.

The Everything® Kids' Sharks Book by Kathi Wagner and Obe Wagner, copyright © 2005 by F+W Media, Inc., ISBN 13: 978-1-59337-304-7, ISBN 10: 1-59337-304-X.

The Everything® Kids' Soccer Book, 2nd Edition by Deborah Crisfield, copyright © 2009 by F+W Media, Inc., ISBN 13: 978-1-60550-162-8, ISBN 10: 1-60550-162-X.

The Everything® Kids' States Book by Brian Thornton, copyright © 2007 by F+W Media, Inc., ISBN 13: 978-1-59869-263-1, ISBN 10: 1-59869-263-1.

The Everything® Kids' Travel Activity Book by Erik Hanson & Jeanne Hanson, copyright © 2002 by F+W Media, Inc., ISBN 13: 978-1-58062-641-5, ISBN 10: 1-58062-641-6.

Contents

Chapter 1

ANIMAL KINGDOM

Caribou Moves

As the seasons change, this herd of caribou moves from the forest to the tundra, looking for food. Can you find your way through the herd? Pick up the letters along the way to spell out the nine-letter word for this seasonal wandering.

Polar Playroom

A mother polar bear digs a den in the snow where she will have her babies and take care of them for several months. She often digs a playroom so her cubs will have room to move around. This mother bear seems to have gotten carried away with her digging! Can you show the cubs the way back to their mother?

START

END

START

Army of Arms

Each of these four creatures has a head surrounded by tentacles or arms. While an octopus has only eight, a nautilus can have more than eighty! Can you make it from **START** to **END** through this grasping group without getting caught?

E
2

T
8

octopus

D
10

squid

E
9

D
1

H

O
7

Squid

Funny Family

These creatures all belong to a family with an odd, but descriptive, name. What is it? Break the letter code and find out! Write your answer on the lines provided.

E
4

D

A
3

Nautilus

Cuttlefish

O
6

F
5

These creatures belong to the

_ _ _ _ _ - _ _ _ _ _ _
family.

END

A Mountain What?

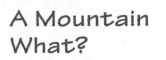

The Mountain Goat is not really a goat at all. To find out what type of animal it is, find the correct path up the mountain from **START** to **END**. The letters on the rocks along the way will spell out the answer.

END

START

The Scavenger

A squirrel spends most of its life gathering food. What it doesn't eat immediately, it hides for later. First, find this squirrel's acorn stash by traveling from **START** to **END**. Then, see how many other acorns you can find hidden in the woodpile!

EXTRA FUN:
How many little snails can you find sliding along the branches?

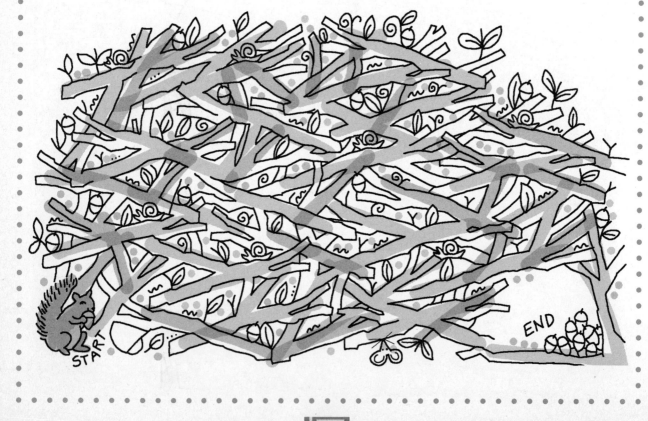

START

Find the Oasis

An oasis is an area in the desert that always has fresh water. Many creatures rely on this precious resource. Can you help this sandgrouse find her way to the oasis? First she will have a long drink. Then she will soak her breast feathers, and bring water back to her chicks!

END

Why Did the Lion Cross the Grassland?

Find your way from **START** to **END**, collecting the letters. When you read them in order, you will discover the answer to this riddle:

Why did the lion cross the grassland?

Smooch!

A prairie dog town is a maze of tunnels that can stretch for acres across the prairie. To keep from ending up in the wrong burrow, these little critters hug and kiss each other when they meet to make sure they are from the same family.

Can you help this little dog find his way home for a smooch?

END

Hello Up There!

The tallest trees in the rainforest stand about 130 feet tall or more. The tops of these trees get the most sunshine, while only a little sunlight reaches the forest floor. Different plants and animals live at different levels in the forest. This scientist wants to study the butterflies who live at the very top of the tallest trees. Can you help her find a way up?

START

Once Upon a Time . . .

NOW

Many species of animals that used to live on Earth don't exist here anymore. Work backwards through the maze from the crocodile (**NOW**) to its ancient relative, the Deinosuchus (**THEN**).

E
E
X
E
X
T
C T T X E
I T N
I N N
C I C N C N
C C

THEN

Collect letters along the path to spell a word that describes species that no longer exist.

C
E
C E T
E T

Giant Anteater

A giant anteater is pretty smart. It doesn't destroy an ant or termite nest that it might find. The anteater will break it open, eat just a little bit, and then go find another nest. This way the ants or termites won't move away to a new nest, and the anteater can come back and eat more, later. This is how the anteater makes its own chain of supermarkets!

Find the seven ant nests that this anteater will be snacking on today. Visit them all, from **START** to **END**.

- In this maze, your path can cross back over itself.
- The correct path leads from the bottom of the nest all the way up to the anthole.

That's A-Maze-Ing!

The giant anteater can stick its tongue in and out more than 150 times a minute! Can you figure out how many times a second that is?

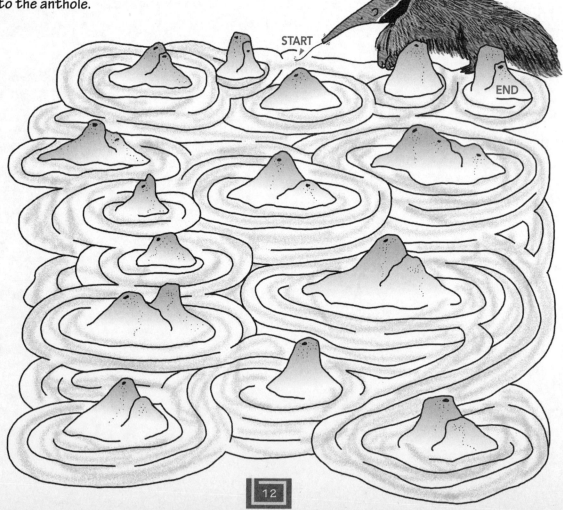

START

END

Green Vine Snake

This snake will drape himself between the vines of a tree. By keeping his tongue still, he looks just like one of the vines. This is a good way to sneak up on a lizard. When the vine snake gets close to his "lunch," he uses special grooves in his snout to judge how far it is. Then—ZAP!

First find the little lizard who is being stalked by a vine snake. Then follow the vines to the lizard and warn him!

END

START

Flying Squirrels

The flying squirrel uses a wide flap of skin stretched between the front and back legs to help it glide. By raising and lowering the flaps (sort of like an airplane), the squirrel can make wide, gentle turns. But, unlike an airplane, the squirrel can also make sharp, right-angle turns in midair! Then, just before landing, the squirrel curves its tail up and uses it like a brake so it lands on the tree trunk with its head pointing up—no airplane can do that!

Flying squirrels come out after dark, so use your night vision to figure out which path will get this graceful glider from tree to tree.

That's A-Maze-Ing!

Most flying squirrels glide for only a few feet. However, the giant flying squirrel can travel more than 1,300 feet (400 meters) between trees!

Where's the Giraffe?

You wouldn't think that an animal almost 20 feet tall could disappear, but giraffes can! How do they do it? Their wonderful brown spots are the secret. You see, where a giraffe lives there are lots of tall, skinny, brownish trees. The sun shining through the leaves creates many moving splotches of shadow and light. A tall, spotted giraffe standing under the trees blends right in!

There are two different paths in this maze. They both start at the word START, and they both end up at a giraffe's hoof. But there are eight hooves to choose from! Which two hooves will you reach?

 **That's A-Maze-Ing!**

A giraffe has only seven bones in his six-foot-long neck—that's the same number of bones as in your neck! What is even more amazing is that a tiny sparrow has 14 bones in his itty bitty neck!

START

15

Terrific Turtles

Turtles belong to a group known as "chelonians." These creatures first appeared on earth about 200 million years ago, making them the oldest living group of reptiles. Modern turtles look almost the same as their ancient relatives. However, the first turtles had small teeth to help them rip their food, while turtles today use the edges of their sharp jaws instead. Also, ancient turtles could not pull their heads into their shells. That's definitely a design improvement that modern turtles have!

Help this musk turtle climb up the branches and out of the water so it can bask in the sun.

END

That's A-Maze-Ing!

Musk turtles sometimes climb into the slanted trees overhanging a river and drop into passing canoes!

16

Chapter 2

LET'S GET SPORTY

Fans Have Fun

Football fans really get into cheering on their team! Can you find your way from **START** to **END** through the crazy crowd?

Move the Ball

Dribble your way around the cones from **START** to **GOAL**. Avoid bumping into other members from your team who are practicing at the same time.

Super Soccer

The game of soccer didn't have one set of rules until the 1800s. Before that time it was a popular game in many English schools, but each school had slightly different rules. However, all the schools agreed on one thing—the ball could never be touched by the player's hands. That's why in England, and in many other countries, the game we call soccer is still called "football"! Help the player with the ball run around the defense to score.

GOAL

That's A-Maze-Ing!

Games in which balls are kicked have been popular for centuries. Early balls were made from all sorts of things—solid balls of rubber or wood, balls of straw wrapped with wool and feathers, even pig bladders!

How do you get to the Baseball Hall of Fame?

To find the answer, follow the correct path from **PLAY BALL** to **GAME OVER**.
Collect the letters along the way, and write them in order on the lines below.

_ _ _ _ _ _ _ ! _ _ _ _ _ _ ! _ _ _ _ _ !

Why does everyone want spiders on their baseball team?

Pick up letters as you find the correct way through the web and around the bases from **HIT** to **HOME RUN**. Write them down in order and you will learn the answer to this riddle!

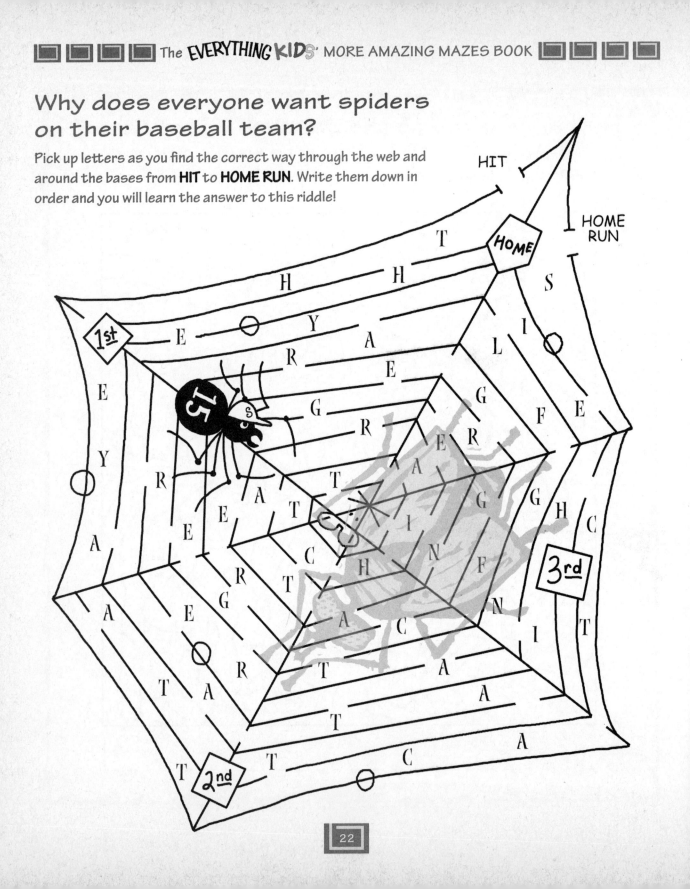

Goofy Golf

Giorgio loves to play goofy golf. You will, too! Here are the rules:

- You must go to every hole.
- Count the dots you hit along each path. Each dot is worth 5 points.
- Add the value of the hole.
- You get a 20-point bonus on any hole with an even-numbered score.

Snake

Windmill

Penguin

Flamingo

Spin Your Wheels

Many of the first bikes were made entirely of wood—even the wheels! These stiff, heavy inventions were so painful to ride on bumpy roads that they got the nickname "bone shakers." Inventors tried to make the ride smoother by giving bikes an enormous front wheel. This did make the ride a bit more comfortable, but it also made bike riding more dangerous. If a rider tried to stop short on one of these "high wheelers," he could easily flip the whole bicycle over and land on his head!

Use this modern mountain bike to reach the top of this very bumpy hill.

END

START

Get on Board

Skateboards were invented by surfers as something to ride when there weren't any waves! The first skateboards were made of wood with metal, rubber, or wooden wheels. These boards were heavy, and it wasn't easy to do tricks on them. But after the invention of fiberglass boards, plastic wheels, and great suspension, skateboarding has become a popular stunt sport that thousands of people enjoy today.

Surf your way through the skateboard park.

START

END

25

Flip a Flying Saucer

Everybody loves throwing a plastic flying saucer around the neighborhood park! They really do look like something from outer space when they're spinning and whirling around in the air. The famous Frisbee™ flying saucers were first made when college students flipped around pie plates that the Frisbee baking company used to bring pies to their cafeteria. The pie plates were recreated in plastic and the flying toy was named "frisbee," after the baking company and their pie plates!

That's A-Maze-Ing!

When the Frisbee inventor's idea was first sold to a toy company, they called it the "Pluto Platter" because the flying disk looked like a UFO!

Find a path that leads right to the mouth of one playful puppy.

START

Rigorous Rock Climbing

Even if a mountain has been climbed before, someone always wants to try a new way. Climbers who wanted to reach the top of Trango Tower decided to use only their bare hands and feet. This peak goes straight up 3,000 feet, which is like trying to climb up the side of a 200-story office building! These climbers used ropes only to catch them if they fell. They climbed by gripping tiny flakes of rock no thicker than a dime with their toes or fingertips, or by jamming their hands and feet into cracks and hauling themselves up.

Follow the cracks and ledges that will lead you to the top of Trango Tower.

That's A-Maze-Ing!

It took nine weeks to reach the top of Trango Tower. Where did the climbers sleep? If they were lucky, they found a tiny ledge on which to pitch their tents. Otherwise, they hung their tents, stoves, and sleeping bags right from the face of the stone. Sometimes the bottom of their tents would be thousands of feet from the ground below!

END

START

Chapter 3

FEROCIOUS CREATURES

Shell Game

Many soft-bodied creatures that used to live in the ancient seas evolved into creatures with hard shells. These shells were good for two reasons: they gave the sea creatures much more protection, and they turned into excellent fossils! Find your way through this fossil shell maze from **START** to **END**

Ptiny Pterosaurs

Some of the smallest pterosaurs were so lightweight that they had to be careful to keep their wings folded when they were resting. Otherwise, the wind could blow them right off their perch! Can you help this pterosaur catch a dragonfly for dinner?

Why Did the Dinosaur Cross the Road?

Find the correct path for this dinosaur from **START** to **END**. Pick up letters along the way that will spell the answer to this riddle.

Heap of Hammers
Find your way from **START** to **END**

START

END

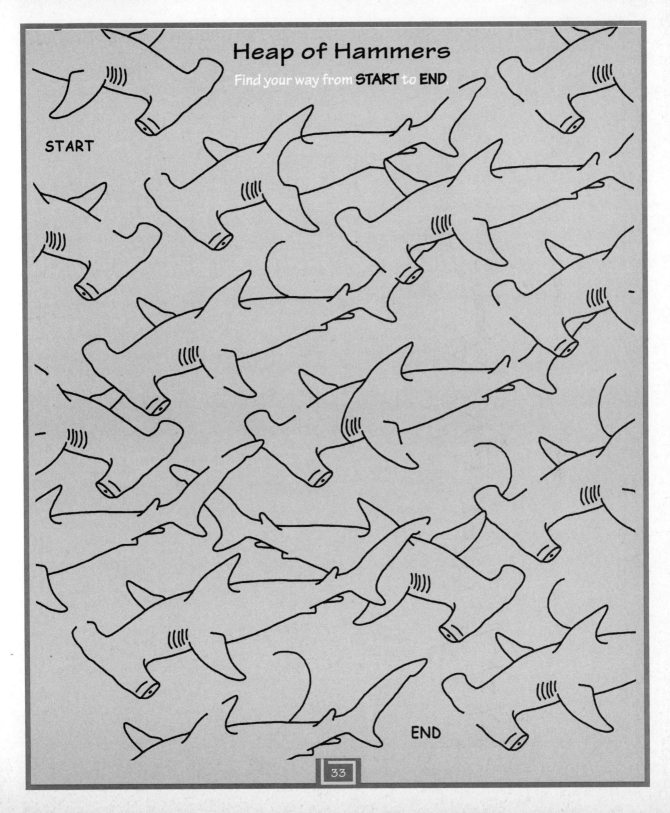

Why did the shark cross the ocean?

Find your way from **START** to **END**. When you have found the correct path, read the letters in order to get the answer to the riddle.

START

END

Frozen Forests

Not all dinosaurs lived in hot climates. About 100 million years ago there were dinosaurs that lived in polar regions! These dinosaurs had to develop special ways to survive long, cold winters. Leaellynasauras (lay-el-ee-nay-SAUR-us) were small dinosaurs, but had huge eyes to help see in the darkness. That's a good thing, because in those icy regions 24-hour-a-day darkness could last for 6 months!

Several leaellynasauras want to gather together. Make one path that ends up going past each dinosaur's head on the way to the center. Don't retrace or cross your own path!

Different Dragons

You probably know about the greedy, wicked dragon who stars in many fairy tales. This dragon lives alone, steals treasure, and burns up the countryside. But did you know that the dragon of Chinese stories is smart, kind, and helpful? The Chinese dragon is part of a very civilized dragon empire that is responsible for taking care of all the water in China!

Find the path that leads to a picture from the book Jimmy is reading. A picture of a messy cave full of treasure means the story is about a wicked dragon, but an underwater palace full of pearls means the story is about a Chinese dragon!

That's A-Maze-Ing!

A long time ago in China, people believed that clear crystals of quartz (a type of rock) were actually solid chunks of dragon's breath!

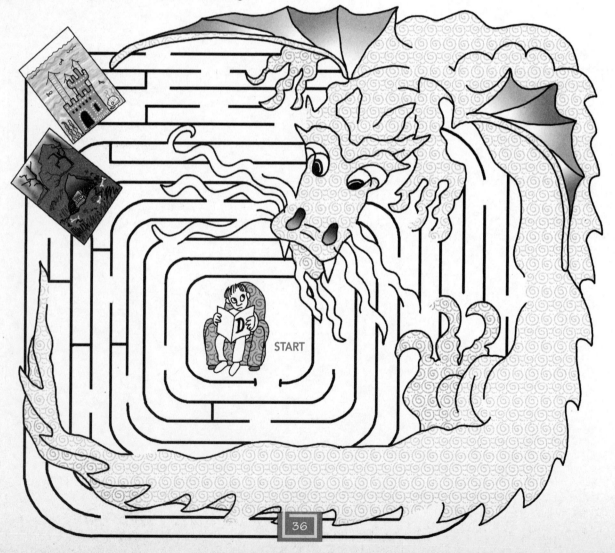

START

Great Griffins

A griffin was supposed to be a powerful creature with the head, front feet, and wings of an eagle, but the body, hind feet, and tail of a lion! Stories say the griffin would fly through the mountains searching for treasure. When he found it, he would stare at the gold for hours, watching it glitter. Griffins were supposed to love look-ing at gold so much that they became the guardians of the troll's gold mines in the mountains!

Follow this griffin to the chest of glittery gold coins.

END

START

Phenomenal Phoenix

Legend says that there can only ever be one phoenix bird! This one phoenix will live for 500 years, and eat nothing but air. Finally, it will build a nest and wait for the rising sun. When the first rays of the sun hit the nest it will burst into flames, and the phoenix will burn into a pile of ashes while singing a beautiful song. But don't worry—three days later, a new phoenix will fly out of the ashes!

Find your way through the nest, through the flames, and out the beak of the singing phoenix.

START

END

Creature Feature

Lots of late-night monster movies feature a slimy green monster that rises out of the ocean, crashing and smashing everything in its way. Of course, these monsters are supposed to be scary not silly, but it is hard not to laugh when you can tell that the monster is a man in a rubber suit, and the cars and buildings are tiny models. However, the movie makers do have a sense of humor—the name of one famous monster is a Japanese slang word that means "big clumsy ox!"

Get the taxi to the park before it gets stepped on!

START

END

Chapter 4

RACECARS
AND
CONSTRUCTION
ZONE

Down and Dirty

The first racetracks weren't the smooth black ovals of today. They were just dirt. This sure made for a rough and bumpy ride! Find the one path that goes from **START** to **FINISH**, missing the bumps and ruts along the way!

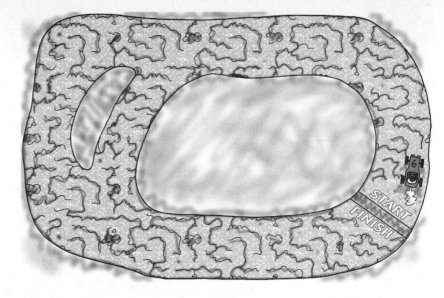

Fans in the Stands

Can you find your way from START to END through these funny fans?

Get Me to the Race

Transporters are an important, and costly, part of every race team. These fifty-foot long giant rigs haul cars, tools, parts, and crew back and forth across the country to all the races. In addition to the cost of the transport equipment itself (easily $300,000 per rig), there are also the costs of food and gas along the way. This can be an additional $100,000 in expenses a year!

Help this transporter make its way from **Race 1** to **Race 2**. You can travel over and under other roads, but this big rig can't make sharp turns. Smooth curves only!

Traffic Jam

Too many fans are trying to get to the racetrack at the same time. Can you help the van full of fans find the "back way" and beat the traffic to the parking lot?

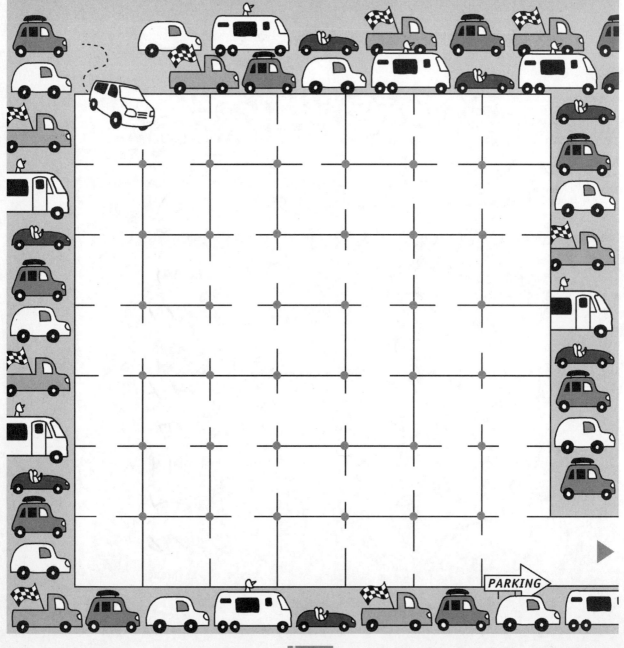

PARKING

Pass in the Grass

One of the most famous saves in NASCAR history was at the Winston 500 in 1987. With ten laps to go, Bill Elliott bumped Dale Earnhardt, Sr.'s car onto the grassy infield. Everyone thought he would spin out and crash, but Dale kept control, drove through the grass, and got back onto the track. He not only saved his car from a wreck, but he won the race!

Help Dale's car (#3) through the infield and back onto the track.

Double Trouble

Two friends are trying to guide their radio-controlled cars through this obstacle course. Can you help them each find a path from **START** to **FINISH**? Here's the tricky part—the paths can't cross each other!

START

FINISH

Mega Wins

NASCAR driver Tony Stewart holds the record for the most money won in a single season. To learn how much he made in 2005, find your way through the maze from **START** to **FINISH**. Add up the numbers you can get to from the correct path and you will see just how successful Tony was that year. Write your answer in the money bag!

Tight Spaces

A skid steer loader is a small construction vehicle that can turn around in very tight spaces. It does this by slowing down or stopping the wheels on one side while the wheels on the other side continue to turn. Help this driver maneuver out from the center of this construction site. At which corner will he end up?

What is it?

Add the missing lines and collect the letters in the maze to find the name for this mighty earth mover.

What do you get when you take a

CRAWLER TRACTOR

and add a

BLADE

to the front?

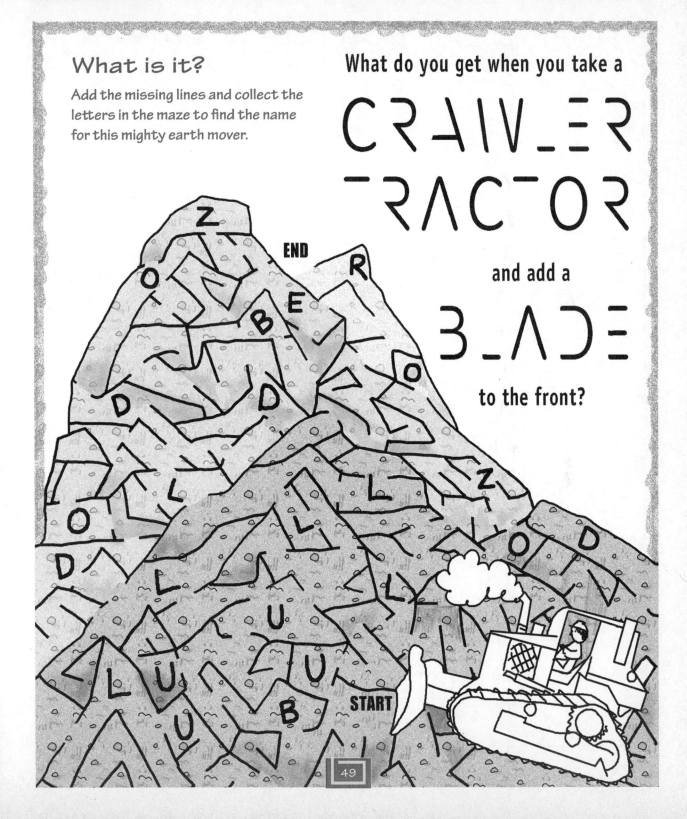

END

START

49

Crazy Maze

This boy has been watching too many big machines. All the pounding, mixing, and shaking has made him dizzy! Help him make it safely through this wild maze.

START

END

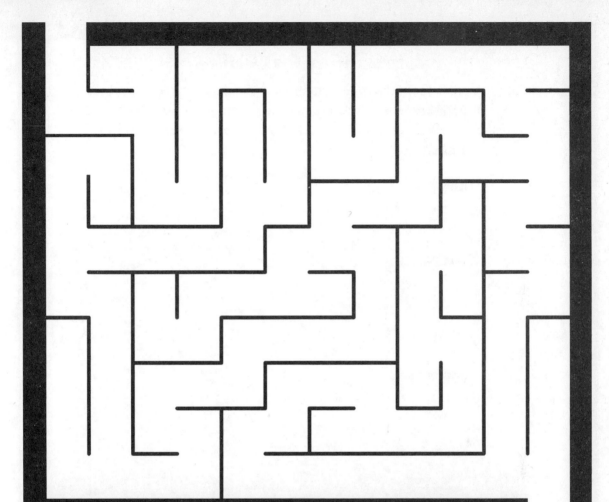

High and Low

The heavy equipment used deep in coal mines are specialized versions of their cousins above ground. Up top, the driver of a giant dump truck will haul coal while sitting in a cab 20 feet in the air. Down below, the driver of a coal shuttle will be sitting just two feet above the tunnel floor. Sometimes the mine is so low that a shuttle driver has to lie down while he is driving! Help this coal shuttle wind its way up to the surface to unload.

Patching Potholes

Potholes are holes in the road caused when chunks of the roadway break away. They can become very deep and cause damage to cars that do not avoid them! Help the road crew work their way over and under through the maze, patching all the potholes along the way.

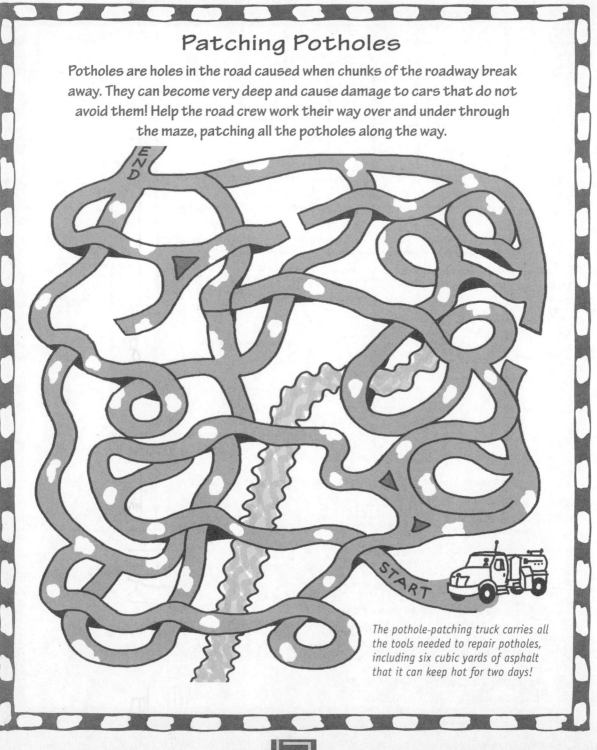

The pothole-patching truck carries all the tools needed to repair potholes, including six cubic yards of asphalt that it can keep hot for two days!

All Clear

Before a structure can be demolished, a thorough check is done from top to bottom to make sure that no one is in the building!

START

Start in the attic and work your way through the house. You must find a path through each room, including the front porch and the basement!

END

Chapter 5

IT'S IN THE PAST

Queen's Favorite

Sir Francis Drake was an English explorer and privateer under Queen Elizabeth I. For years and years, he had his government's permission to attack and rob Spanish ships. How did his country reward his piratelike behavior? Break the Flip-Flop Code to find out.

START & END

That's A-Maze-Ing!

Sir Francis Drake is also known as the first Englishman to sail around the globe! Can you find the path that leads all the way around his portrait, and back to the beginning?

Nasty Knots

A large pirate ship could have several miles of rope, or "rigging," to hold up the sails, and lots more rope to tie down the cargo. That meant pirates needed to know, and use, hundreds of different kinds of knots. One wrong turn, and a sail could come crashing down, or the precious cargo could slide overboard!

**Unfortunately, this new pirate has tied a terrible knot!
Follow the rope over and under to find the correct way to untie it.**

ARRRR!
What'n the
devil be
this mess?

AWWWK!
That's not
a knot!

START

END

Scrub-a-Dub-Dub

Help the pirate scrub his ship from **STERN** (very back) to **PROW** (very front).

STERN

PROW

Get a Grip

Pirates threw a grapnel, or grappling iron, onto the ship they were attacking. The hooks got caught in the rigging and made it easier for the pirates to pull the ship close so they could jump on board! Can you find your way through this tangle from **START** to **END**?

Standing Room Only

The hanging of a pirate was a public spectacle. Huge crowds came to the gallows to watch the event. Can you find your way through this crowd and up to the noose?

OOPS! The pirate that was supposed to be hanged has escaped! Can you see him in the crowd?

END

START

Going Up!

The native Chachapoyas of Peru hid their mummies high on cliffs that jutted out of the jungle. The Chachapoyas were very smart because down lower where they lived it was cool, wet, and rainy. High above the treetops the cliffs were warm and dry—perfect for mummies! **START** at the bottom of the cliff and climb until you can enter the tomb.

START

THAT
TO
THAT
HIS
HE
STATUE
AN
WOULD
EYE
UGLY
MAKE
HUNGRY
SCARE
SO
SO
IN
WAS
AND
EVIL
GODS

Small Protector

Bes was a very short god who had a potbelly, a beard like a lion, and was often shown with his tongue sticking out! His important jobs were to protect women and children and guard the home, especially at night. Many houses had a statue of Bes near the front door. Why? Travel through the maze from **START** to **END**. Read the words along the path to learn about this god's surprising way of doing his job!

WAS
UGLY
SPIRITS
HE
HE
HE
START
END
TO
AWAY

Ba Humbug!

Ancient Egyptians believed that when a person died, his or her unique spirit, or "ba," was set free. This spirit would go looking for the person's life force, or "ka." The ba could only search for the ka at night. During the day it had to return to the mummy of its person! The ba looked like a small bird with the face of the person it belonged to. Match this ba to the correct mummy and get him home as quickly as possible. Hurry up, the sun is rising!

Hide and Seek

The pharaohs of ancient Egypt were buried in a special tomb called a pyramid. These huge buildings were built from blocks of stone that could weigh up to two tons each! The pharaoh was buried deep inside the pyramid in a special chamber full of gold, jewels, and expensive offerings. It is not surprising that robbers wanted to break in to steal the treasure! For this reason, pyramids had many fake burial chambers and passages that were dead ends. These were supposed to confuse the robbers and keep the treasure—and the pharaoh—hidden.

Can you find your way to the hidden chamber that protects the pharaoh's mummy?

START

Float by Boat

All the stones used in the pyramids had to be brought to the building site from stone quarries. Some limestone could be found nearby, but other stones, like granite, came from far away. Stones were cut at quarries, loaded onto barges, and floated down the Nile to the building site. Steer the barge from the stone quarry to the dock closest to the pyramid.

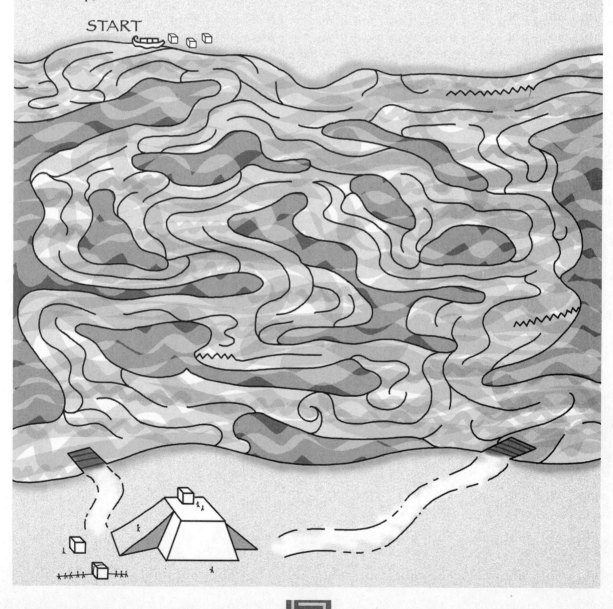

OOPS!

Some fascinating explorers didn't reach their goal. In 1915, Ernest Shackleton was heading to Antarctica when his ship became trapped by ice. For ten months the ice-locked ship drifted, and was finally crushed. The crew saved three lifeboats and made it to an empty island. Most of the crew camped there while Shackleton and five men tried to reach the nearest town, 800 miles away. After sailing for two weeks through stormy seas, with 30-foot waves threatening the tiny lifeboat, the rescuers landed. After a 20-mile hike and a scary slide down a 1,000-foot cliff of ice, Shackelton and his men reached the town. By the time Shackleton returned to the island to get the others, five months had passed!

Help Shackleton's new ship find a safe passage through the ice.

START

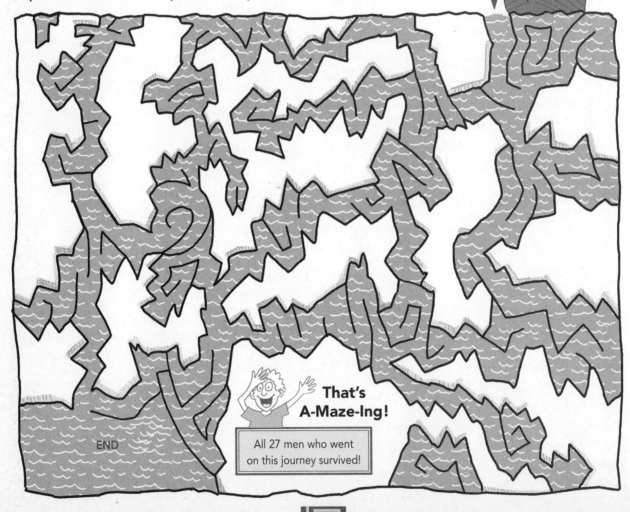

END

That's A-Maze-Ing!

All 27 men who went on this journey survived!

Flying Tigers

END

The Flying Tigers is another name for the "American Volunteer Group" who flew during World War II. Even though their old and battered planes were always short of fuel and parts, the Flying Tigers used speed, surprise, and precision flying to score victory after victory.

Get the Flying Tigers through the enemy planes.

START

That's A-Maze-Ing!

The front of each Flying Tiger plane was painted to look like an open mouth full of sharp teeth—but they were shark teeth, not tiger teeth!

67

Checkmate

Knights liked to play the game of chess because it is a game of war and strategy. Chess pieces are named for the people and places that were common in the life of a knight. There is the king, queen, bishop, pawn (or foot soldier), castle, and, of course, the awesome knight on his horse. Do you know the best part of chess? A tired knight didn't have to put on his armor to play!

Help this brave chess knight cross the board to capture the enemy king.

END

START

The Royal River

Egypt is lucky to have the Nile river snaking right through the center of its driest desert. For the ancient Egyptians this meant a beautiful place to live and grow food. Because cities were built close to the water, the Nile was also used as a giant highway. Boats traveled up and down the river with food, merchandise, and visitors. In fact, the Nile was such an important part of daily life, that many wealthy people were buried with models of boats, so they could continue to float on the Nile in their next life!

The pharaoh's son is playing by the busy river. Find a safe path for his toy boat.

Sacred Cats

Ancient Egyptians were crazy about cats! Not only did they rely on cats to keep mice away from their grain, but they used cats to help them hunt and enjoyed them as special pets. They even had a goddess named Bastet who had the head of a cat. This friendly goddess was always ready to play and dance— just like a real cat! When a favorite cat died, the owner might have the body mummified so the cat could "enjoy" a beautiful afterlife. Hundreds of cat mummies were found in the Egyptian city of Bubastis, where there was a large temple to honor Bastet!

Can you find your way through the elaborate linen wrapping of this honored cat mummy?

That's A-Maze-Ing!

Ancient Egyptians would show their sadness over the death of their cat by shaving their eyebrows!

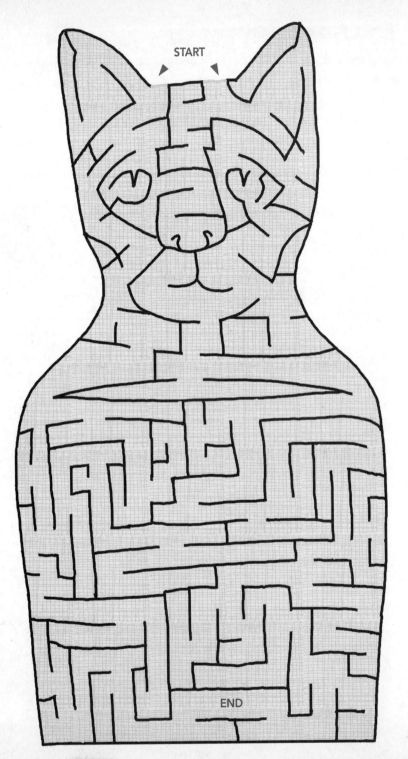

START

END

Chapter 6

DAY BY DAY BY DAY

Super Separates!

See how fast you can get each item through the maze and into the proper recycling bin. The only rule? Paths may cross each other, but may not travel together. Here's the fun part — there is more than one way to do this puzzle!

PAPER   **CANS**   **BOTTLES**

Ants

Help the ants find their way across the blanket to the picnic. Stop at all the sweet treats, but go past the silverware.

Start

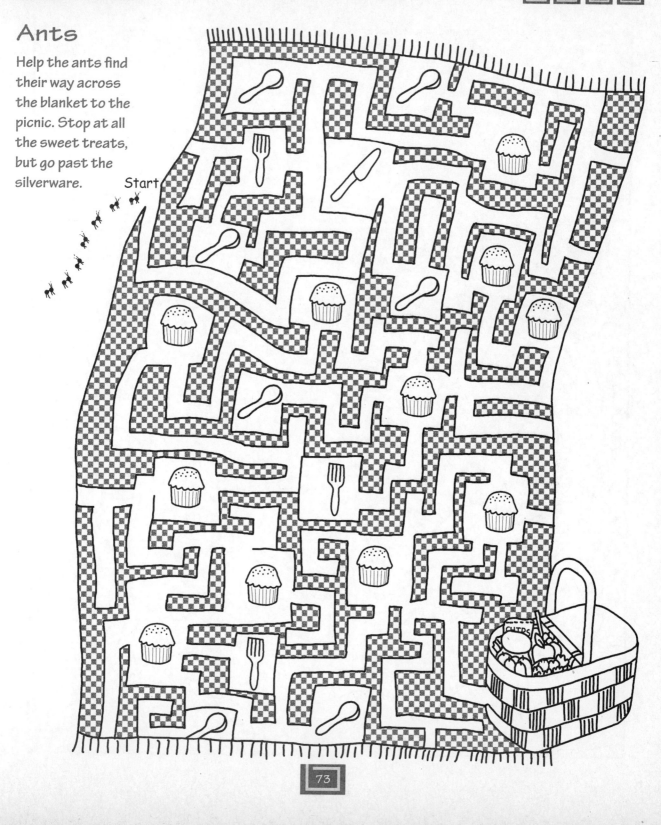

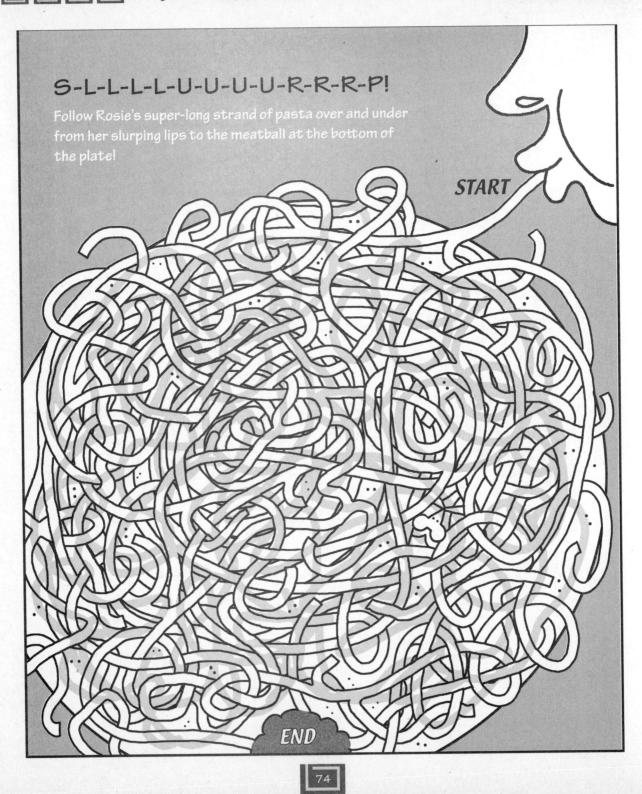

S-L-L-L-L-U-U-U-U-R-R-R-P!

Follow Rosie's super-long strand of pasta over and under from her slurping lips to the meatball at the bottom of the plate!

START

END

Whoooosh!

Hurricane Harriet scattered Pat's Hat Shop! Can you help put it together again? Start here and find a path that collects the sign, roof, awning, and door. Return them here to the store.

EXTRA: See if you can find the 35 hats that Pat lost!

Beep Beep

The Dot family has spent the day at a giant craft fair. Now it's time to go home, but where is their car? Look around carefully—Papa Dot had it painted a special way, and even got a special license plate. Can you spot the Dots' car, and find the family a path to it?

Peanut Butter and . . . ?

You may like peanut butter sandwiches with jelly or marshmallow. But some people like peanut butter with more unusual foods! Complete each of the food items below with letters from the word PEANUT BUTTER.

_ O L O G N _

_ O _ _ _ O CHI _ S

CHOCOL _ _ _

B _ CO _

CH _ _ S _

_ ICKL _ S

M _ S _ _ _ D

_ _ _ _ SL _ Y

M _ YO _ _ _ IS _

O _ IO _

_ . _ . Q. S _ _ C _

START

END

EXTRA FUN: Munch your way through this unusual sandwich from **START** to **END**. Find any strange ingredients?

Poll your friends—which P.B. combo is their favorite?

Mouse in the House!

Have you ever had a mouse in the house? Sometimes they get in through your basement, or if someone leaves the backdoor open for too long. You'd better hope you have a cat around to help you chase it out! But remember, you're much bigger than the mouse—he's probably much more afraid than you think!

Help this mouse find his way through the mess in the basement to the other side of the room, where there's cheese at the door—before the cat catches him! After you have found the correct way, trace over the path with a brightly colored crayon or marker. Does your path make a picture?

START

Bouncing Ball

Those colorful rubber bouncy balls you can find in toy stores, party favor bags, and vending machines can go crazy when they're bouncing down a set of stairs. The rubber balls come in a thousand different sizes, colors, and designs—see how many you and your friends can collect. Be careful using the balls in the house, though!

Follow one bouncy path from the top to the bottom of the stairs.

Crazy Crayons

Crayons were originally made in Europe around the 1700s and were imported into this country at a high price. Nowadays, crayons are made in the United states by mixing a few types of waxes, such as paraffin, beeswax, and carnauba wax. The waxes are melted in a huge pot. Workers then add colored powders to make thousands of different shades. Today you can find so many varieties of crayons—basic colors, neon shades, multicolored crayons, and crayons with glitter inside!

That's A-Maze-Ing!

In 1996, the Binney & Smith Company produced the 100 billionth Crayola™ Crayon!

Start coloring the path with one crayon. Fill in the whole path from side to side. When you come to a dot, switch colors. Do this all the way to the center.

How many different colors do you think it will take to get to the middle of this maze?

Creative Clay

Did you know that you can make your very own clay at home, using just flour, water, and a few other common foods? Have an adult help you make the following recipe. Use the food coloring to get different colored clay, then sculpt you own creations!

You Will Need:
1 cup flour
1 cup water
½ cup salt
1 tsp. vegetable oil
Food coloring

Directions:
Have the adult mix all the ingredients in a saucepan and cook over medium heat (stirring constantly) until the mixture holds together. When the clay is cool enough to touch, start kneading and rolling!

Follow each clay "snake" back into its can! Your path will go over and under.

Board Game-a-Rama!

If you step into any toy store, you're likely to find hundreds of board games stacked to the ceiling! There are games for kids of all ages, and for all types of interests—money, sports, trivia, strategy, and animals, just to name a few. Some games are simple and some require more thinking or planning. With all these choices, you're bound to find one you like. It's a great idea to play board games with your family and friends on rainy days, or when the computer is broken!

Oh no—the crazy cat has knocked over the game board! Find your way to the dice and start the game over. HINT: You can travel on different shades of blue, but can't cross the dark blue lines.

Chapter 7

EW, GROSS!

There's a Fungus among Us

A mushroom is a kind of plant called a fungus. Believe it or not, there is one kind of fungus that loves to hang out on the skin of your feet—especially between the toes. All it needs is a good food supply (like some tasty dead skin cells) and some moisture (sweaty sneakers are great) and this foot fungus can go crazy. Pretty soon you'll have a case of itching, burning, smelly athlete's foot!

START

END

Z-Z-Z-Zombies

AAARGH!! They look like sleepwalkers—shuffling slowly, arms outstretched, no expression on their faces. The only difference is they are coming to get YOU! And once they do, they will either eat your brains, or turn you into a zombie just like they are. Since zombies are already dead, how do you stop them?

START by renting a zombie movie. Watch it all the way to the **END**!

START

END

85

Scoop the Poop!

Everyone knows that dogs gotta go—too bad many
dogs go where people also like to run and walk!
Can you find the path that helps the soccer player
reach the **END** of the game while dodging the doo-
doo? Even better, find a second path that **END**s up
scooping four of the six plops. Make sure the two
paths do not cross over each other.

soccer
player
start

pooper
scooper
start

END

END

START

ACHOOO!

Dust, pollen, germs, and all kinds of floating crud are constantly trying to bash their way into your body. But they have to make it through the heavily guarded nose first. If the tissue lining the nose gets too irritated, the body will quite literally explode—with a sneeze! Traveling up to 100 mph, a sneeze will blast thousands of dirty droplets back out of the nose and away from the body. Phew!

87

Itchy Scratchy

What's the size of a sesame seed, has six legs that end in claw-like hooks, and can't survive for more than a day without a meal of human blood? Meet the common head louse. If your hair happens to be infested with these critters, you'll want to get rid of them quickly—each female can lay up to 100 eggs!

START combing. See how many lice you **END** up getting rid of!

START

END

Scorpion Soup

Many people would shriek if they saw a scorpion in their kitchen. But in some parts of the world scorpions are cooked into a tasty soup! Grab a spoon and see if you can find your way through this serving. Be careful not to eat the tips of the tails!

END

START

Tasty Termites

If you ever travel to Singapore, be careful what you eat for appetizers. A gourmet snack is a live termite queen (2 inches or longer are the tastiest). Not sure about eating live termites? OK, travel to South Africa where you can get your termites fried in oil and served with tomato!

START with a termite and **END** with a quick bite!

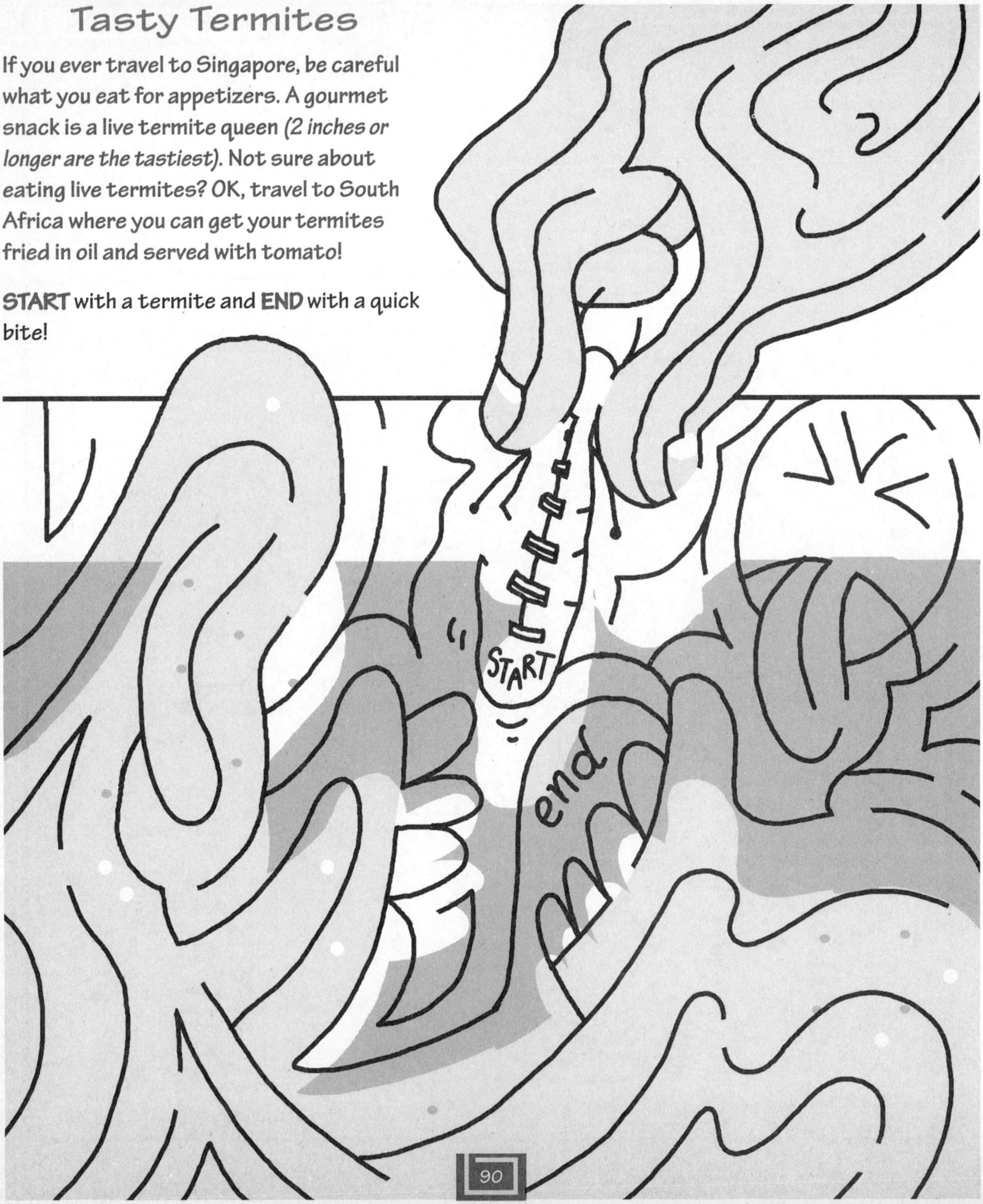

START

end

Sewer Diver

The poop, pee, and everything else from 20 million people all flow into the ancient sewer system of Mexico City, Mexico. The liquid that sloshes through the huge pipes is so murky and full of "stuff," even a spotlight can't cut through it. So what happens if a pipe gets backed up? A trained diver puts on a special diving suit, is lowered deep into the sewers, and feels his way through the sludge until he reaches the clog. What will he find . . . a bicycle, a basketball, or a dead body? Would you want to find out?

Chapter 8

FRIGHTFULLY SPOOKY!

Monster Mash

Let's face it—no matter how hairy, slimy, or sharp toothed, we love monsters! Everyone has spent some part of their allowance on monster stories, monster movies, Halloween monster makeup, and even bendable monster action figures! While most monsters are designed to frighten, others are just plain fun. After all, who could be scared of a monster who only wants to eat cookies?

Can you help the monster with all the sweet teeth cross the room to the creepy cake?

END

Frankenstein's Monster

One dark and stormy night, a young author went to bed and had a nightmare about a scientist who created a living monster out of assorted body parts he had put together. It took her a year to write down her dream, but Mary Shelley's novel *Frankenstein* was finally published. Mary Shelley was just 20 years old!

Follow the bolt of lightning to the switch that will bring the monster to life.

START

END

That's A-Maze-Ing!

People think "Frankenstein" is the name of the monster. But it is really the name of the scientist that created him. The monster is simply called "the monster"!

Who Are Jekyll and Hyde?

The Strange Case of Dr. Jekyll and Mr. Hyde is a story about a scientist who invents a potion to separate his good personality (Jekyll) from his evil one (Hyde). Unfortunately, the destructive Mr. Hyde becomes so strong that the good Dr. Jekyll can't keep him under control. The story is a very popular subject for horror movies. In fact, at one point there were ten different movie versions of *Dr. Jekyll and Mr. Hyde*!

Find your way through the boxes from **START** to **END**, and watch the transformation of gentle Dr. Jekyll into his evil counterpart, Mr. Hyde.

That's A-Maze-Ing!

It's hard to imagine that the author of *Dr. Jekyll and Mr. Hyde*—Robert Louis Stevenson—also wrote *Treasure Island*, about pirates, and *A Child's Garden of Verses*, a book of children's poems!

 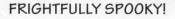
Wild About Werewolves

The ancient people known as Vikings may have fought with the first "real" werewolves. The Vikings told stories of warriors who were amazingly fierce. These warriors, called "berserkers," would put on shirts made of wolfskin before they went into battle. These "men in wolf coats" were terrifying—they feared nothing, seemed to feel no pain, and fought with superhuman strength. It was probably easy for stories of these real-life warriors to turn into stories of men who actually turned into wolves.

There are also many stories about people who turn into wolfmen when the moon is full. Can you make it across the face of this full moon before the werewolf howls?

START

END

That's A-Maze-Ing!

The word "berserk" is still used today to describe someone who goes completely out of control!

Burning Bonfire

Bonfires were often used to scare evil spirits away. Find your way from **START** to **END**, through the burning flames, to banish this evil spirit.

END

START

Piece of Pie

Pumpkin pie is especially good with a swirl of whipped cream on top. Can you eat your way through this piece of pie from **START** to **END**?

START

END

Any Body Home?

See if you can find your way from start to end through this totally haunted house. Try not to run into any of the spooky inhabitants!

Eek: What happens when a ghost stubs his toe?

Meek: He gets a boo-boo!

START

THE END

All Wrapped Up!

Tommy was dying to be a mummy for Halloween. His Dad helped out by wrapping him from head to toe in toilet paper. Can you find your way from **START** to **END**?

START

Mumbling Mummy

Fill in the missing letters for all these words that rhyme with **MUMMY**.

Sticky and chewy.
__UMMY

Another word for stomach.
__UMMY

Not very good.
__ __UMMY

Delicious!
__UMMY

END

Looking for Letters

Follow the letters to spell out what trick-or-treaters might
chant as they go door to door on Halloween.

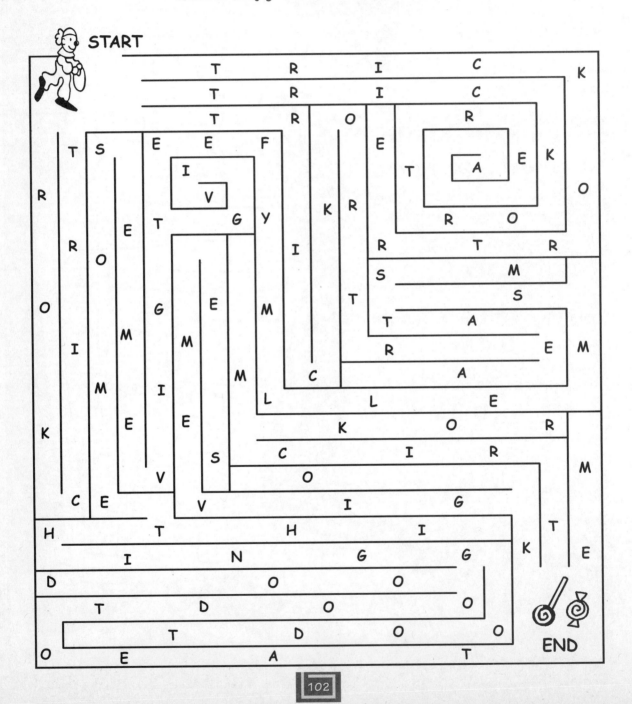

Short Cut

Are you sure this is the right way home?
See if you can find the right path.

Heads Up!

Ride from **START** to **I'M OVER HERE!** to help the legendary headless horseman find his head.

I'M OVER HERE!

START

Flying Foxes

"Flying Foxes" are actually the largest of all bats. They can have wing-spans of up to four feet, and bodies the size of a small house cat! However, this bat isn't a monster-movie bloodsucker. Even though it looks scary, the Australian flying fox is a gentle eater of fruit, blossoms, and nectar. Flying foxes like to gather together during the day—sometimes there are as many as a million bats in one place!

See if you can wiggle your way through this crowded bat camp.

END

START

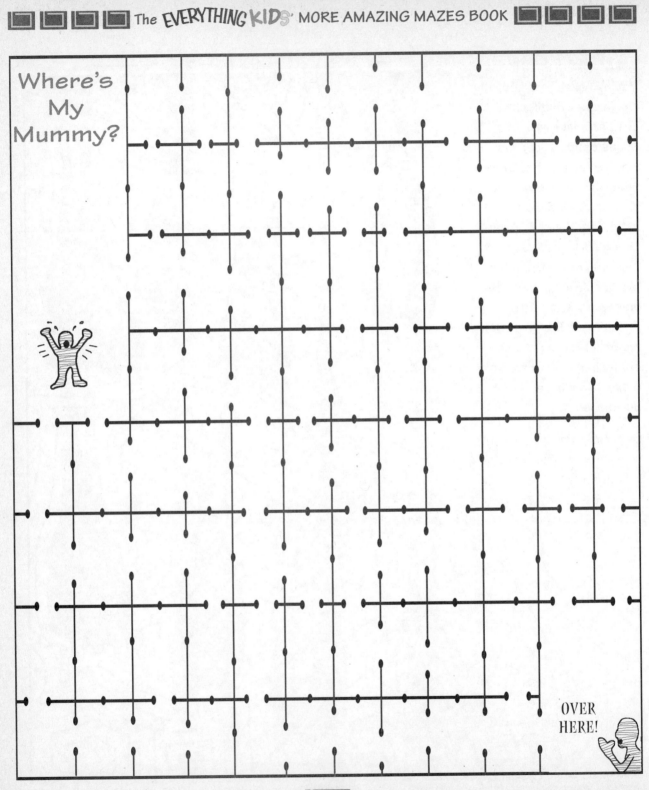

Where's My Mummy?

OVER HERE!

Chapter 9

EXTRA FUN!

Pony Express

START with this letter in Missouri and see how quickly you can deliver it to the **END** in California!

START

Missouri

END

California

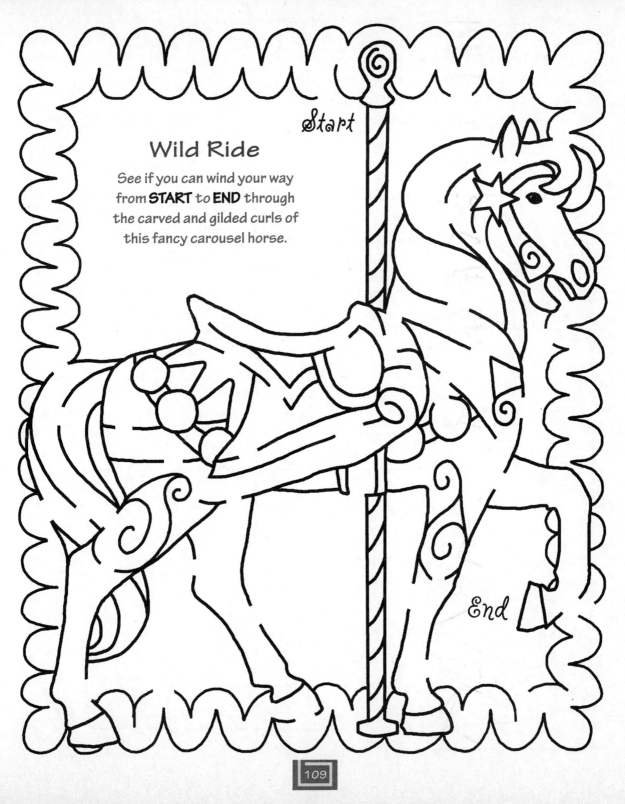

Wild Ride

See if you can wind your way from **START** to **END** through the carved and gilded curls of this fancy carousel horse.

Yee Ha!

They were handcrafted in Concord, NH, but were famous for carrying mail and passengers throughout the western United States! Can you help this Concord Coach deliver the mail from **START** to **END** of the route?

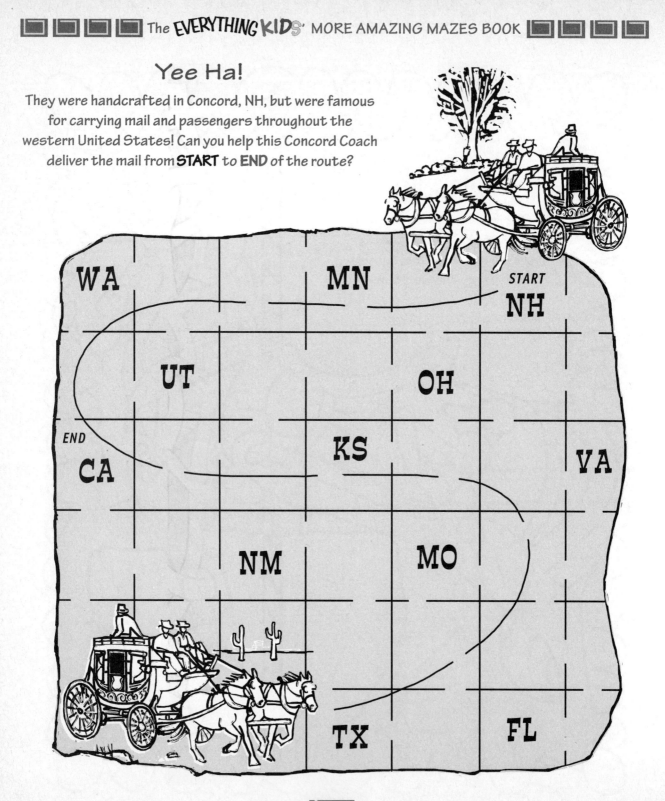

Crossing Indiana

Indiana has more interstate highways per square mile than any other state. Maybe that's why its state motto is "The crossroads of America"!

See if you can find the one route that **ENTER**s and **LEAVE**s Indiana. You can travel over and under on the roads, but must stop at road blocks or dead ends!

ENTER

LEAVE

Crazy Cities

Driving around an old city can be like time traveling. Today's roads might have started out hundreds of years ago as walking trails or as horse paths. These paths might have twisted to follow a river, or maybe they made a sudden turn to miss a huge tree or rock. As more people, buildings, and, finally, cars came to the city, these simple trails were paved and new roads were added. Over many years, some cities have ended up with a confusing maze of roads!

Your family has planned a fun day in downtown Tobson. **START** at the playground, then figure out how to drive to:

1. The Aquarium
2. The Public Gardens
3. The Museum of Science

HINT: Go to each place in order. Watch out for one-way streets (marked by arrows), or streets blocked by barriers.

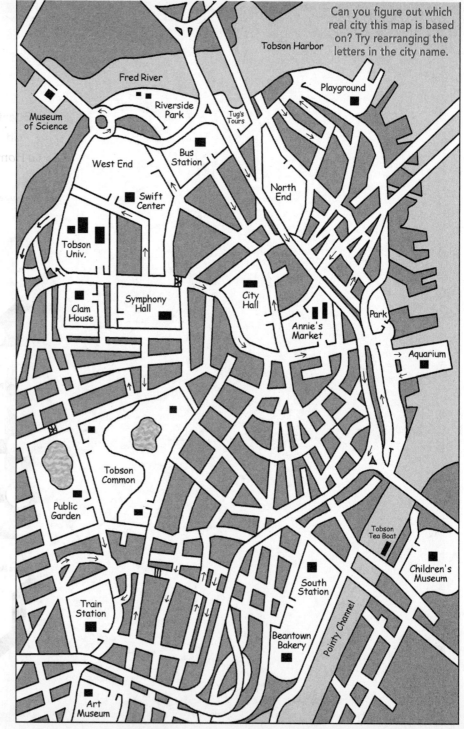

Can you figure out which real city this map is based on? Try rearranging the letters in the city name.

Super Subways

Subways seem like a modern city convenience, but believe it or not people in London, England, were riding the first subway in 1863—that's over 130 years ago! New York City didn't get a subway system until 1904, but now it has the largest in the word with 239 miles of track. With so many different stations and routes to choose from, it's a good thing that the subway companies print free maps!

Your family has bought an all-day pass to ride the Silver City subway. Starting at Home Court station, find the quickest way to travel to these other stations (in order): City Place, Sports Center, Prince George Plaza, Crystal City, Green Park. Phew! Now head back to Home Court.

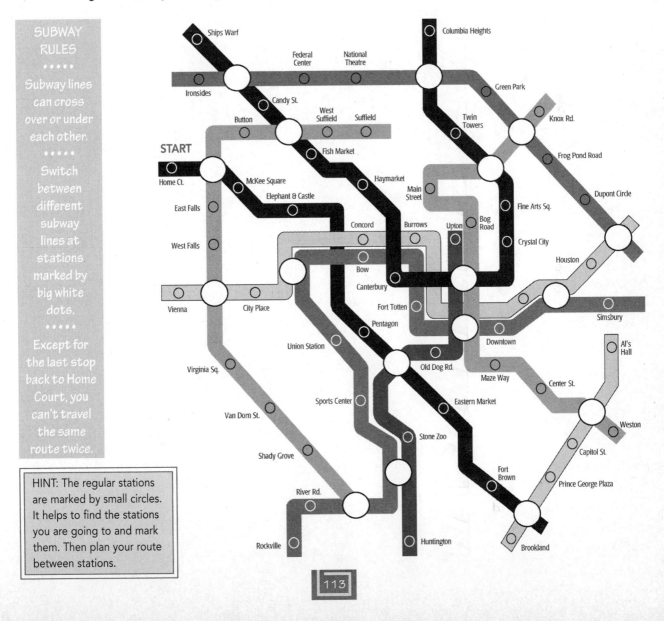

SUBWAY RULES
· · · · ·
Subway lines can cross over or under each other.
· · · · ·
Switch between different subway lines at stations marked by big white dots.
· · · · ·
Except for the last stop back to Home Court, you can't travel the same route twice.

HINT: The regular stations are marked by small circles. It helps to find the stations you are going to and mark them. Then plan your route between stations.

Appendix A

PUZZLE
ANSWERS

page 2 • Caribou Moves

Answer: M I G R A T I O N

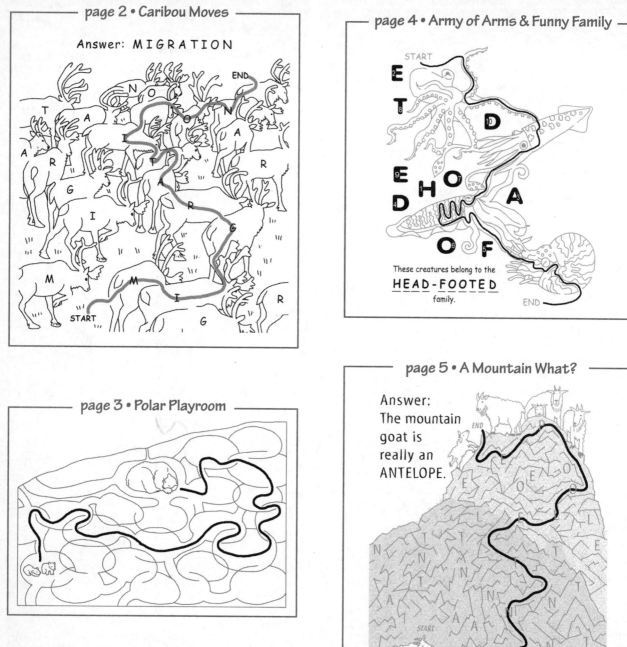

page 3 • Polar Playroom

page 4 • Army of Arms & Funny Family

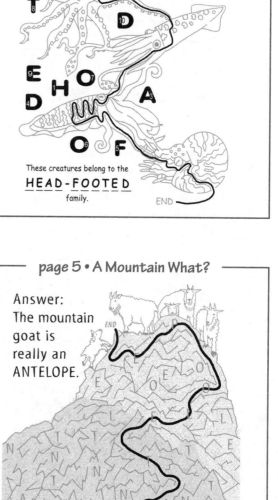

These creatures belong to the
HEAD-FOOTED family.

page 5 • A Mountain What?

Answer:
The mountain
goat is
really an
ANTELOPE.

page 6 • The Scavenger

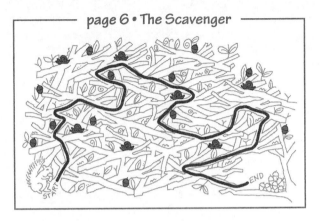

page 7 • Find the Oasis

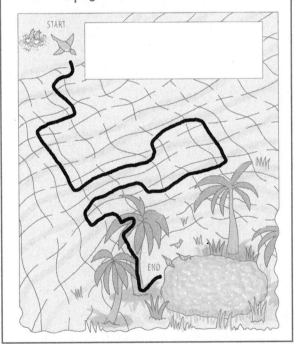

page 8 • Why Did the Lion Cross the Grassland?

Answer: To get to the other pride!

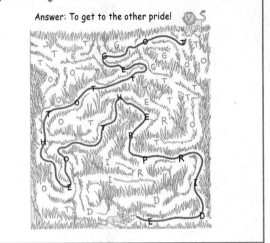

page 9 • Smooch!

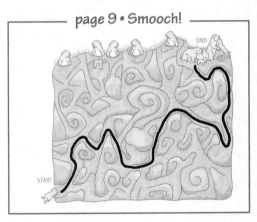

page 10 • Hello Up There!

page 11 • Once Upon a Time . . .

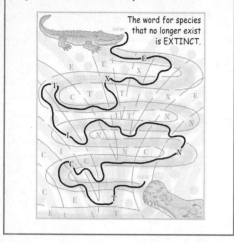

The word for species that no longer exist is EXTINCT.

page 12 • Giant Anteater

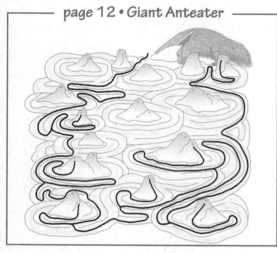

page 13 • Green Vine Snake

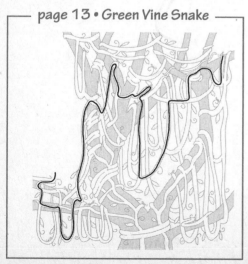

page 14 • Flying Squirrels

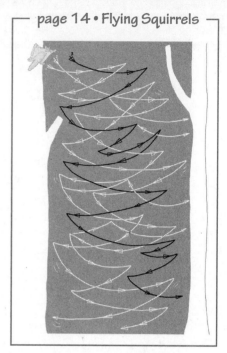

page 15 • Where's the Giraffe?

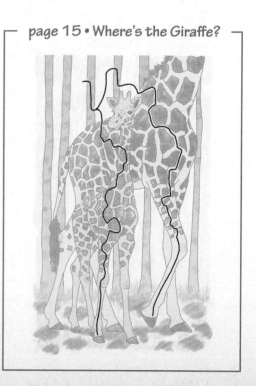

page 16 • Terrific Turtles

page 20 • Super Soccer

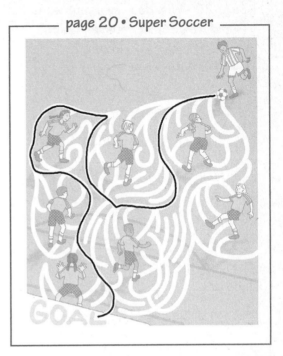

page 18 • Fans Have Fun

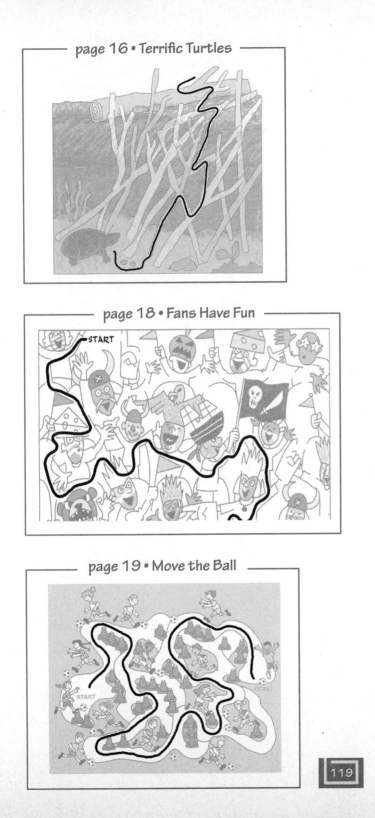

page 21 • How do you get to the Baseball Hall of Fame?

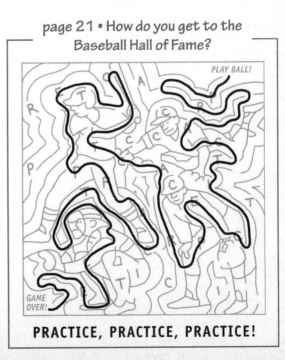

PRACTICE, PRACTICE, PRACTICE!

page 19 • Move the Ball

page 22 • Why does everyone want spiders on their baseball team?

THEY ARE GREAT AT CATCHING FLIES!

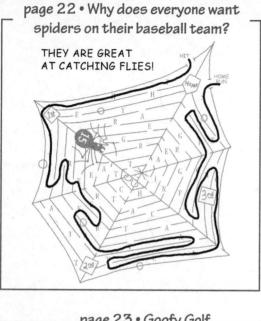

page 23 • Goofy Golf

Snake: 153 pts. (no bonus)

Penguin: 147 pts. (no bonus)

Flamingo: 122 pts. + 20 pt. bonus = 142

Windmill: 114 pts. + 20 pt. bonus = 134

page 24 • Spin Your Wheels

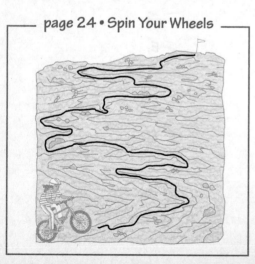

page 25 • Get on Board

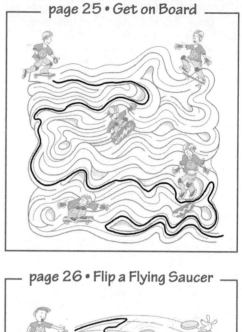

page 26 • Flip a Flying Saucer

page 27 • Rigorous Rock Climbing

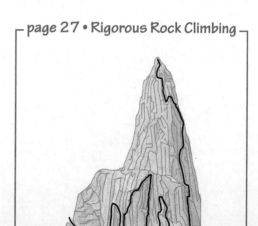

page 30 • Shell Game

page 31 • Ptiny Pterosaurs

page 32 • Why Did the Dinosaur Cross the Road?

Because chickens had not evolved yet!

page 33 • Heap of Hammers

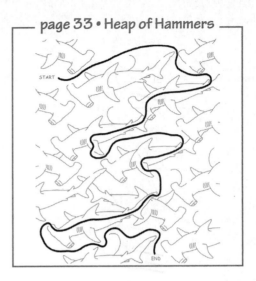

page 34 • Why did the shark cross the ocean?

ANSWER: To get to the other tide!

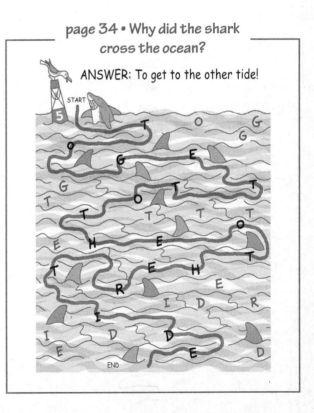

page 35 • Frozen Forests

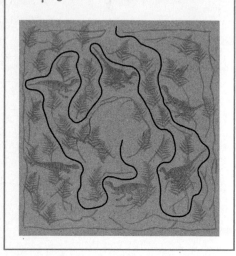

page 38 • Phenomenal Phoenix

page 36 • Different Dragons

page 39 • Creature Feature

page 37 • Great Griffins

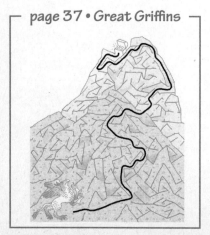

page 42 • Down and Dirty

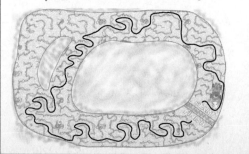

page 42 • Fans in the Stands

page 43 • Get Me to the Race

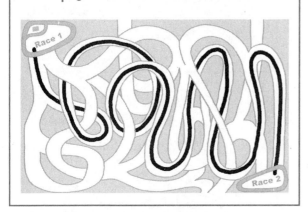

page 44 • Traffic Jam

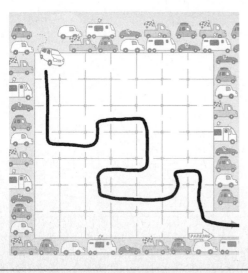

page 45 • Pass in the Grass

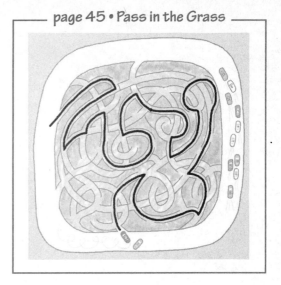

page 46 • Double Trouble

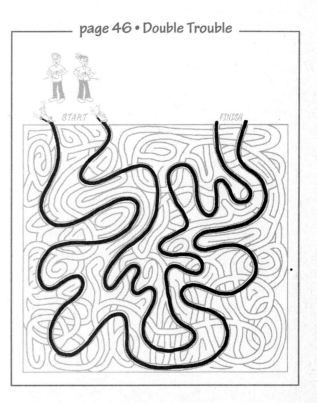

page 47 • Mega Wins

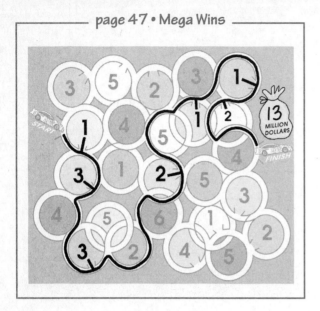

page 49 • What is it?

ANSWER: BULLDOZER

What do you get when you take a

CRAWLER TRACTOR

and add a

BLADE

to the front?

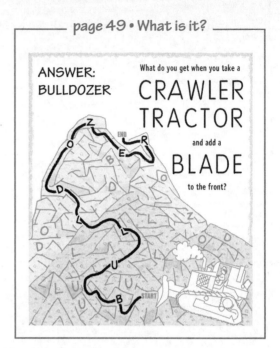

page 48 • Tight Spaces

Just so you know: A "multi-terrain loader" is a skid steer loader with treads *(like a tank)* instead of wheels.

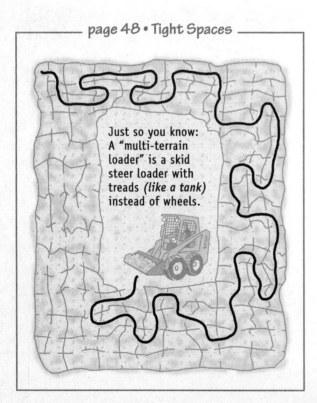

page 50 • Crazy Maze

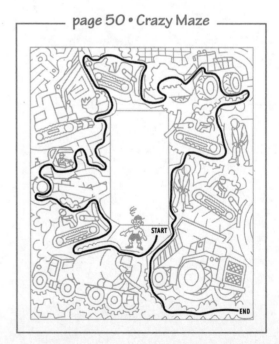

page 51 • High and Low

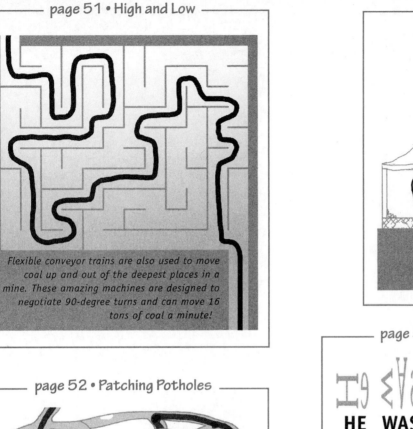

Flexible conveyor trains are also used to move coal up and out of the deepest places in a mine. These amazing machines are designed to negotiate 90-degree turns and can move 16 tons of coal a minute!

page 53 • All Clear

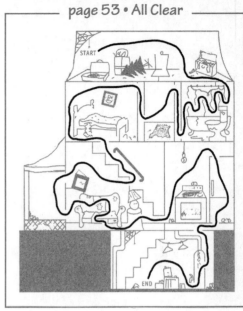

page 52 • Patching Potholes

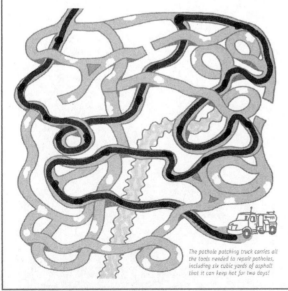

The pothole patching truck carries all the tools needed to repair potholes, including six cubic yards of asphalt that it can keep hot for two days!

page 56 • Queen's Favorite

HE WAS MADE A KNIGHT

page 56 • Queen's Favorite

page 57 • Nasty Knots

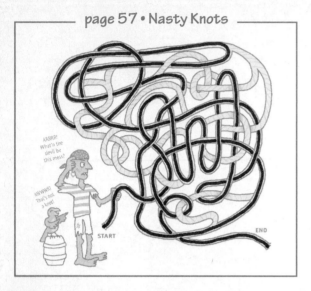

page 58 • Scrub-a-Dub-Dub

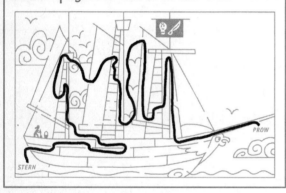

page 59 • Get a Grip

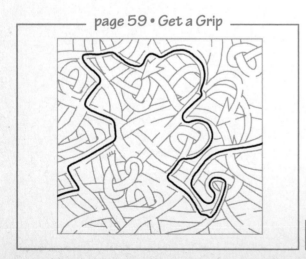

page 60 • Standing Room Only

page 61 • Going Up!

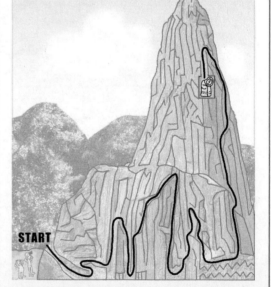

page 62 • Small Protector

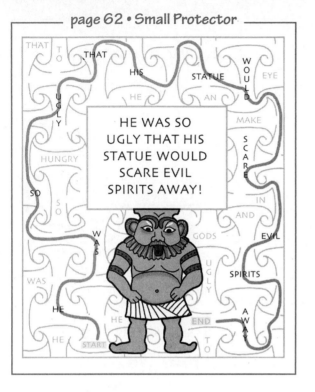

HE WAS SO UGLY THAT HIS STATUE WOULD SCARE EVIL SPIRITS AWAY!

page 64 • Hide and Seek

page 63 • Ba Humbug!

page 65 • Float by Boat

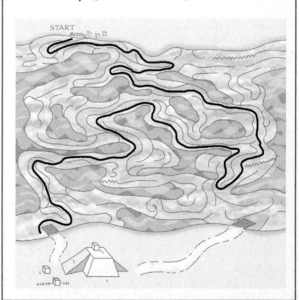

page 66 • Oops!

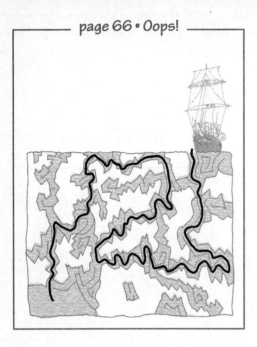

page 68 • Checkmate

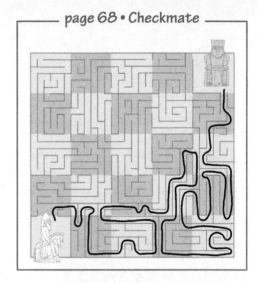

page 69 • The Royal River

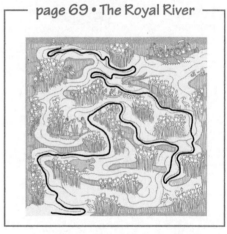

page 67 • Flying Tigers

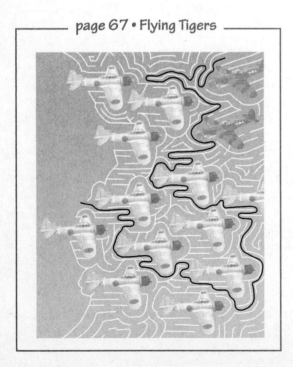

page 70 • Sacred Cats

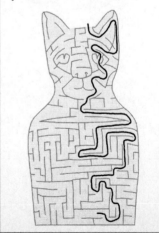

PUZZLE ANSWERS

page 72 • Super Separates!

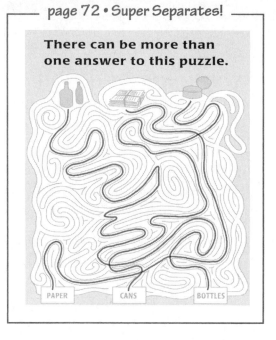

page 74 • S-L-L-L-U-U-U-R-R-R-P!

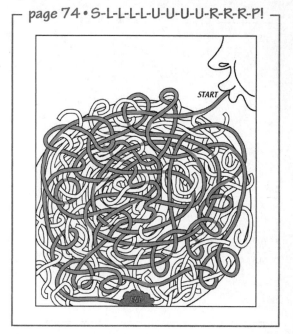

page 73 • Ants

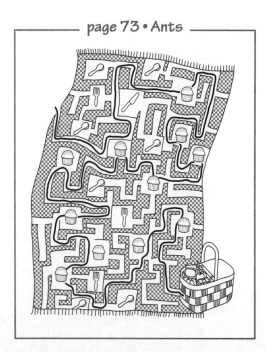

page 75 • WHOOOOSH!

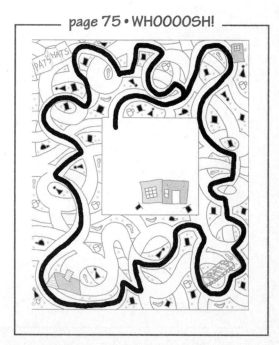

page 76 • BEEP BEEP

page 78 • Mouse in the House!

page 77 • Peanut Butter and . . . ?

B<u>O</u>L<u>O</u>G<u>N</u>A
P<u>O</u>T<u>A</u>T<u>O</u> C<u>H</u>IP<u>S</u>
C<u>H</u>O<u>C</u>O<u>L</u>ATE
B<u>A</u>C<u>O</u>N
C<u>H</u>E<u>E</u>S<u>E</u>
P<u>I</u>C<u>K</u>L<u>E</u>S
M<u>U</u>ST<u>A</u>R<u>D</u>
P<u>A</u>R<u>S</u>L<u>E</u>Y
M<u>A</u>Y<u>O</u>NN<u>A</u>IS<u>E</u>
<u>O</u>N<u>I</u>O<u>N</u>
B.<u>B</u>.<u>Q</u>. S<u>A</u>U<u>C</u>E

page 79 • Bouncing Ball

page 80 • Crazy Crayons

page 82 • Board Game-a-Rama!

page 81 • Creative Clay

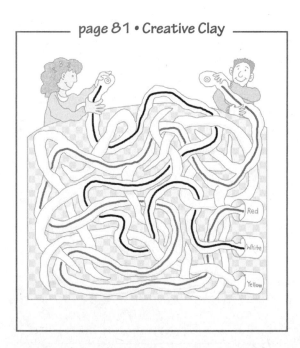

page 84 • There's a Fungus among Us

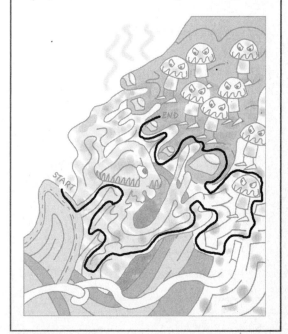

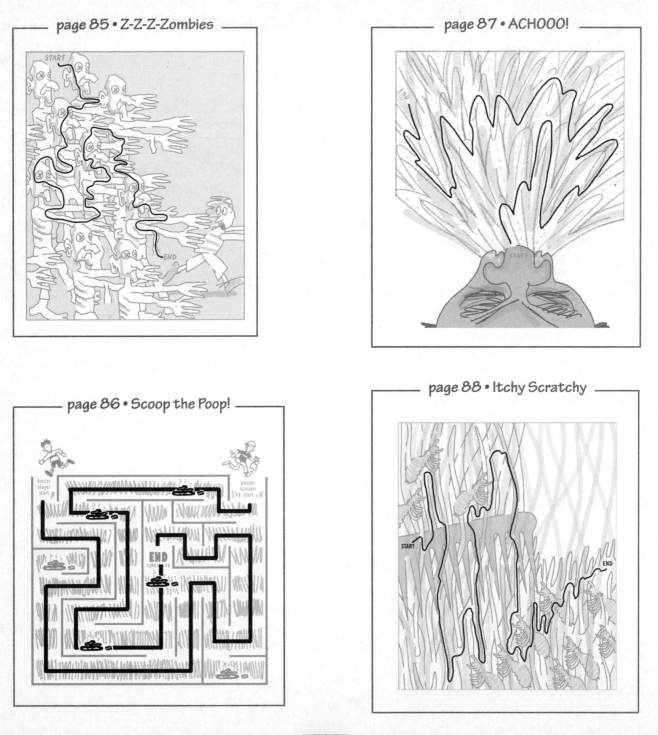

page 85 • Z-Z-Z-Zombies

page 87 • ACHOOO!

page 86 • Scoop the Poop!

page 88 • Itchy Scratchy

page 89 • Scorpion Soup

page 91 • Sewer Diver

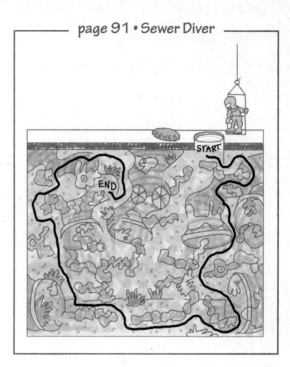

page 90 • Tasty Termites

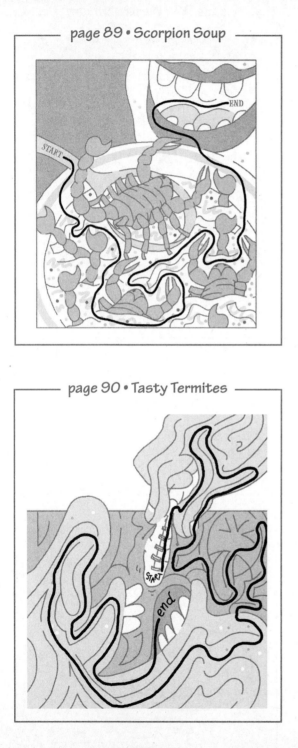

page 94 • Monster Mash

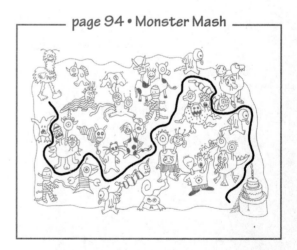

page 95 • Frankenstein's Monster

page 96 • Who Are Jekyll and Hyde?

page 97 • Wild About Werewolves

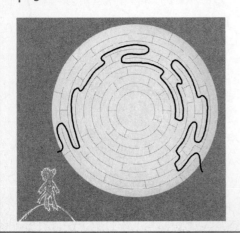

page 98 • Burning Bonfire

page 99 • Piece of Pie

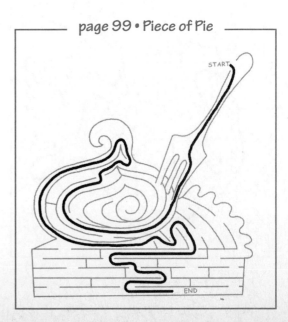

page 100 • Any Body Home?

page 103 • Short Cut

page 101 • All Wrapped Up!

page 101 • Mumbling Mummy

Sticky and chewy.
G UMMY

Another word for stomach.
T UMMY

Not very good.
C R UMMY

Delicious!
Y UMMY

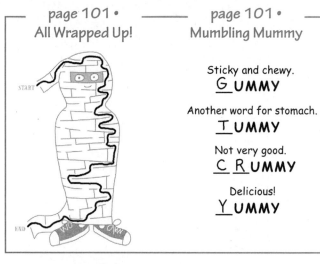

page 104 • Heads Up!

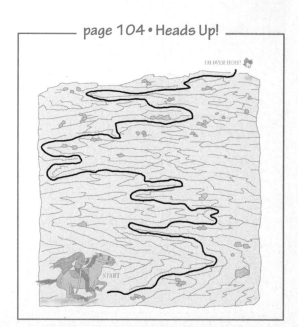

page 102 • Looking for Letters

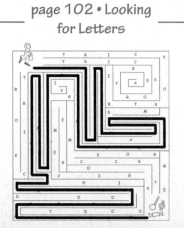

page 105 • Flying Foxes

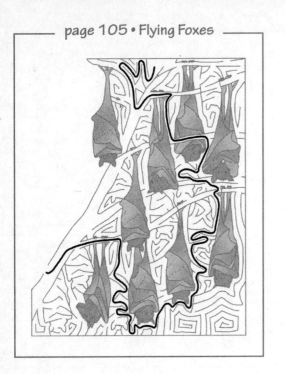

page 108 • Pony Express

page 106 • Where's My Mummy?

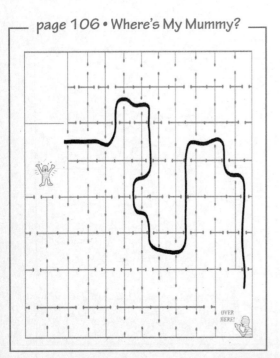

page 109 • Wild Ride

page 110 • Yee Ha!

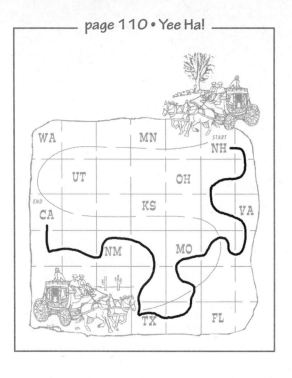

page 111 • Crossing Indiana

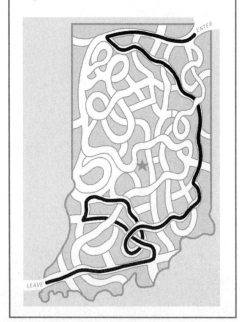

page 112 • Crazy Cities

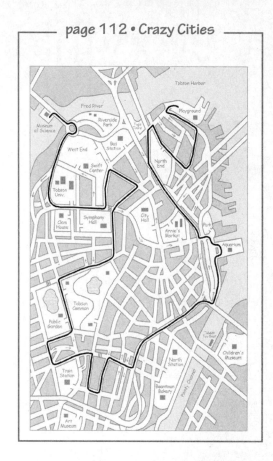

page 113 • Super Subways

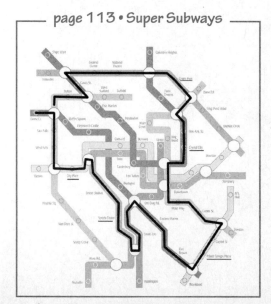

Find out Everything on Anything
at **everything.com!**

The new **Everything.com** has answers to your questions on just about everything! Based on the bestselling Everything book series, the **Everything.com** community provides a unique connection between members and experts in a variety of fields. Since 1996, Everything experts have helped millions of readers learn something new in an easy-to-understand, accessible, and fun way. And now Everything advice and know-how is available online.

At **Everything.com** you can explore thousands of articles on hundreds of topics—from starting your own business and personal finance to health-care advice and help with parenting, cooking, learning a new language, and more. And you also can:

- **Share advice**
- **Rate articles**
- **Submit articles**
- **Sign up for our Everything.com newsletters to stay informed of the latest articles, areas of interest, exciting sweepstakes, and more!**

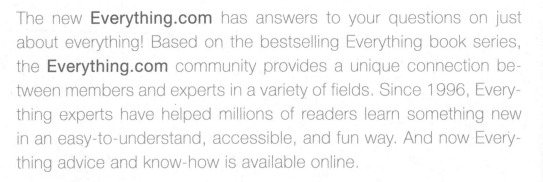

Visit **Everything.com** where you'll find the broadest range and most authoritative content available online!